# Rosa's Animals

## The Story of Rosa Bonheur and Her Painting Menagerie

Maryann Macdonald

Abrams Books for Young Readers
New York

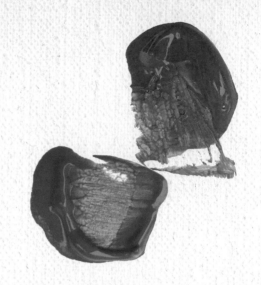

*The paintbrushes incorporated into the design of this book are the same type as those used by James McNeill Whistler, who worked at roughly the same time as Rosa Bonheur.*

Cataloging-in-Publication Data has been applied for and may be obtained from the Library of Congress.

ISBN 978-1-4197-2850-1

Printed and bound in China
10 9 8 7 6 5 4 3 2 1

Abrams Books for Young Readers are available at special discounts when purchased in quantity for premiums and promotions as well as fund-raising or educational use. Special editions can also be created to specification. For details, contact specialsales@abramsbooks.com or the address below.

**ABRAMS** The Art of Books
195 Broadway, New York, NY 10007
abramsbooks.com

For Nicolas and George Ryan

*The Lion at Home*, 1881. Lions became one of Rosa's favorite animals to draw and paint. She visited zoos and circuses so that she could draw and paint leopards, tigers, and monkeys, too.

How many people keep pet lions? The great painter Rosa Bonheur had three: Pierrette, Nero, and Fathma. (Today we know that trying to turn wild animals into pets is a bad idea, but back in the 1800s, in Rosa's time, people didn't think that way.) "Fathma . . . followed me around like a poodle," Rosa said. "She was so tame that I'd let her put two paws around my neck. Then I'd take her head in my hands and kiss her." When Pierrette got sick, Rosa nursed her like a daughter, and the lion died gazing into Rosa's eyes. "To be loved by wild animals," the artist said, "you must love them." And all her life, Rosa most certainly did.

*Rosa at Four*, 1826, by Raymond Bonheur. Along with her doll, Rosa is clutching a drawing pencil.

# Cows and Cats

Rosalie Bonheur—or Rosa, as she was later called—was born in Bordeaux in southwestern France in 1822. As a toddler, she fell in love with the strong oxen, peaceful sheep, and calm cows she saw in the French countryside. "You just cannot imagine how much I loved feeling some fine cow lick my head while she was being milked," she said.

When Rosa was only two years old, her father, Raymond, an artist, wrote in a letter: "Rosa is a dear little thing, and I must tell you that already she has a taste for the arts." She scrawled ducks and chickens in the dirt with a stick. She cut out animal shapes with scissors. Her mother, Sophie, remarked, "I don't know what Rosa will be, but I have a conviction that she will be no ordinary woman." Sophie taught Rosa how to write the letters of the alphabet by drawing a different animal to go with each. The little girl was thrilled to learn about all the creatures!

When Rosa's father went to Paris to find work in 1828, Rosa, then six years old, missed him terribly. "Rosalie asks every day when you are coming back," Sophie wrote to Raymond in a letter. And later she informed him, "Rosalie is sending you in the box her first tooth that has come out and a picture, with the promise of nicer ones in the future." Yet when the family joined Raymond in Paris the following year, Rosa was disappointed by the city. She found it shabby and sad. But across the street from her family's new apartment was a butcher shop with a painted wooden boar standing outside. "I thought he was alive!" she later said.

Soon the silvery pigeons, proud dogs, and prowling cats of Paris caught her eye. But, most of all, Rosa grew to love the patient horses that hauled wagons, carriages, and buses through the city streets in the 1800s. Rosa encouraged her two little brothers, Auguste and Isidore, to play "horse" with her. Together they galloped and cantered and trotted all around the square, now known as the Place des Vosges, near their home.

A horse-drawn bus in Paris, 1828.
Illustrator unknown.

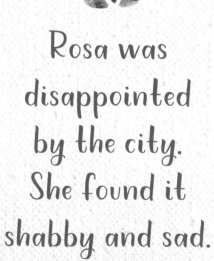

Rosa was disappointed by the city. She found it shabby and sad.

*Boulevard du Temple*, 1838–1839, by Louis Daguerre. This early street photograph was made in Rosa's day not far from where she lived in Paris. It is considered to be the first photograph to show people.

*La toilette, du Saint - Simonien.*

The Saint-Simonians had to help each other get dressed, since their strange uniform (said to have been invented by Rosa's father) laced up the back. Illustrator and date unknown.

In the building where the Bonheur family lived was a school run by a teacher named Father Antin. When Rosa's brothers became his students, Father Antin noticed that Rosa was left without her playmates, and he offered to allow her to attend class with them. Most little girls did not go to school in those days, and almost never with boys. But Rosa's father accepted the teacher's offer on the spot. As Rosa later wrote, "This was, I believe, the first pronounced step in a course which my father always pursued with us children. It emancipated [freed] me before I knew what emancipation was." Rosa was used to playing with her brothers; she liked boys' rough games, and she said she learned early on to use her fists to defend herself!

When Rosa was ten years old, a terrible disease called cholera raged through Paris, killing nearly twenty thousand people. To avoid infection, the family moved away from the crowded city center. In their new neighborhood, Rosa's father met up with the Saint-Simonians, a group of idealistic people who believed, among other things, in the equality of men and women. The Saint-Simonians' ideas appealed to the impulsive Raymond. He soon became an enthusiastic member of the group and decided to go live in their monastery with the other "apostles." His wife was left behind to look after Rosa, Auguste, Isidore, and the youngest Bonheur, two-year-old Juliette. Sophie tried to support the children by giving piano lessons and sewing, and she took them to visit their father whenever she could.

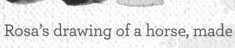

Rosa's drawing of a horse, made when she was about thirteen years old

Facing page: *Self-portrait*, 1823, by Raymond Bonheur. Raymond's nickname during his early days in Bordeaux, where this self-portrait was painted, was "Angel Gabriel." Without her father's training and confidence in her, Rosa could probably not have become an artist.

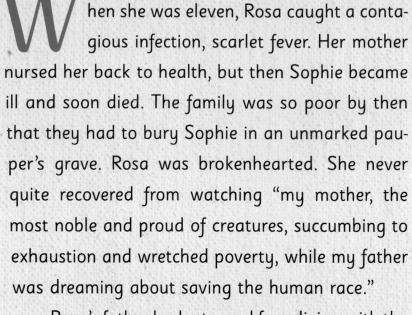

When she was eleven, Rosa caught a contagious infection, scarlet fever. Her mother nursed her back to health, but then Sophie became ill and soon died. The family was so poor by then that they had to bury Sophie in an unmarked pauper's grave. Rosa was brokenhearted. She never quite recovered from watching "my mother, the most noble and proud of creatures, succumbing to exhaustion and wretched poverty, while my father was dreaming about saving the human race."

Rosa's father had returned from living with the Saint-Simonians just before Sophie died. Wanting Rosa to learn a trade, he tried to apprentice her to a seamstress. But sewing bored Rosa. She had too much energy to sit quietly in a chair and stitch seams. So Raymond sent her to boarding school, as he had done with her brothers. "I was a real devil there," Rosa said later. One day, she organized the other children to play "knights on horseback," one of her favorite games, in the school's rose garden. The garden was trampled and destroyed, and Rosa was sent home.

Nothing seemed to calm restless twelve-year-old Rosa except drawing. But most people at the time did not think girls could become artists. Art schools would not even accept them as students. So in 1835, Raymond, who had become an art teacher, decided to make his elder daughter one of his pupils. Rosa was thrilled. "At long last I was going to be able to draw to my heart's content!" she said.

*Rabbits Nibbling Carrots*, 1840 (detail)

# Rabbits, a Squirrel, and a Pet Goat

Like many French painters of his time, Raymond Bonheur was a Realist. Realists believed in drawing and painting the world around them exactly as they saw it. They used everyday life and working people as subjects. This was a great change from the late 1700s and early 1800s, when Neo-Classical artists focused primarily on idealized forms inspired by ancient Greek and Roman art and Romantic painters played on a viewer's emotions. Because Raymond was a Realist, he encouraged his daughter, too, to draw from life, not from her imagination.

Because Rosa loved animals more than anything, she started out drawing and later even sculpting them. To better pursue her studies, she brought some rabbits to live in her father's art studio. She worked hard to sketch their layered fur, pointed ears, and gleaming eyes. At night she attempted to capture the ripples of illumination cast by lamplight on their mottled coats.

When she was fourteen, Rosa went to the Louvre Museum to copy famous paintings and statues. This was a traditional way to train artists in France, but Rosa was one of the youngest students there. "I have never seen . . . such ardor for work," the museum director said of her. But because she was a girl and wore big smocks and pants to work in, some of the other students made fun of her. In turn, Rosa drew silly pictures of them. But why should she care what other people thought? At sixteen, she sold her first painting for one hundred francs—almost as much as an average French worker might make in a month! "What a joy!" she later wrote. "I thought I'd really made it." She was proud to be able to help her father support the family.

Louvre Museum, c. 1865, photograph by
Auguste-Rosalie Bisson

Rosa's cartoon of a copyist

*Joan of Arc at the Coronation of Charles VII,* 1854, by Jean Auguste Dominique Ingres. Ingres was the leading Neo-Classical painter. This painting of Saint Joan, the medieval girl soldier, demonstrates how Neo-Classicists drew from ancient Greek and Roman imagery. Saint Joan appears almost as a statue. The scene idealizes the event.

*Confrontation of Knights in the Countryside,* c. 1834–1842, by Eugène Delacroix. Delacroix was a leading Romantic painter. This painting is filled with energy and tension and arouses the viewer's emotions.

*A Ewe and Two Lambs*, date unknown, by Juliette Bonheur.
Rosa's sister loved painting animal subjects as much as she did.

When Auguste and Isidore returned home from boarding school as teenagers, Raymond Bonheur taught them to paint and draw in his studio with Rosa. Juliette also joined her sister and brothers when she reached her mid-teens. At that point, everyone in the Bonheur family was an artist. The studio became a workshop of sorts, and the children Raymond's apprentices. Raymond would decide on the concept for a work of art, and all the Bonheurs would work on it in the same style, so that the final version would seem to have been executed by a single hand. Eventually, each artist in the family established an individual career while continuing to help the others. Auguste specialized in portraits and landscapes. Juliette began with still lifes and later went on to paint animal subjects, as Rosa loved to do. Rosa, who had also taught herself to sculpt, generously tutored her favorite brother, Isidore, who also became a gifted animal sculptor.

By now, the Bonheurs had many animal "models" living in their studio. Rosa constructed a shelter out of branches and heather for the rabbits, chickens, ducks, and quail. Canaries and finches flew about freely, and rats wandered around at will. A pet squirrel, Kiki, made a nest in the hollow leg of a statue. But one day Kiki gnawed through a cord holding up a heavy painting, and the huge canvas crashed down onto Raymond's easel, destroying a work in progress. After that, Kiki had to live in a cage.

At fourteen, Isidore loved animals as much as Rosa did. He would carry their goat, Jocrisse, down five flights of stairs so that the animal could graze outside. Once, he and Rosa hid inside some water pipes lying on the ground, and Jocrisse sprang from pipe to pipe, peeking inside each to find his friends.

The Bonheur family: Isidore, Juliette, Auguste, and Rosa, photograph by André-Adolphe-Eugène Disdéri. Rosa seems to be the star of the show.

*Goat,* by Isidore Bonheur. Could Rosa's brother have been thinking of their pet goat, Jocrisse, when he sculpted this bronze?

19

Rosa discovered a farm run by a peasant woman just outside Paris, and she spent many happy days there drawing cows, sheep, and goats with shiny horns, soft fur, and sturdy hooves. "I really got into studying their ways," wrote Rosa, "especially the expression in their eyes."

Always begin with a vision of the truth. The eye is the way to the soul, and the crayon or brush must simply and tastefully render what you see.

—ROSA BONHEUR

*Head of a Calf*, 1878

Rosa F. Bonheur 1840

Salon de Paris, 1857. At the Salon, paintings were hung from floor to ceiling. Dressed in the elaborate fashions of the day, people walked the rooms to see works by their favorite artists as well as to discover the new artists included.

Rosa was just nineteen when, in 1841, her painting of two gentle rabbits nibbling on a carrot was accepted for the Salon, a prestigious Paris art show held at the Louvre Museum every year. None of the judges, all famous artists, had anything nice to say about Rosa's painting, however, and it was, sadly, hung in a dark corner. Nevertheless, the very fact that her work was shown at the Salon at all was a great honor. The Salon was *the* place where artists gained fame with both the public and the all-important art galleries that sold paintings.

*Rabbits Nibbling Carrots*, 1840. Even though the painting is damaged, the rabbits still look alert and almost alive.

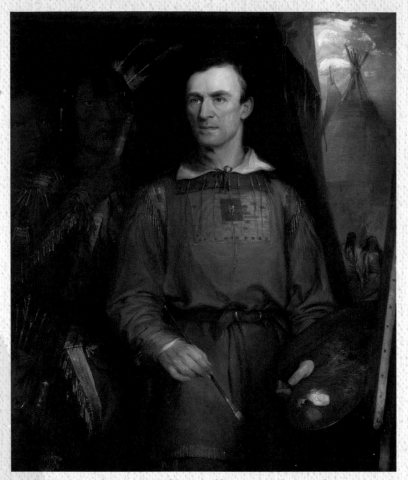

*George Catlin*, 1849, by William Fisk,. Fisk painted this portrait when Catlin was in London.

An American painter named George Catlin was visiting Paris around the time that Rosa's rabbit painting was shown at the Salon. Catlin specialized in scenes of the American West, and he brought a huge collection of his paintings and artifacts he had collected with him to Europe. (He also brought a group of Native Americans and set up a Crow teepee made of twenty-five buffalo skins inside the Louvre.) Two of his portraits were displayed at the 1848 Salon, where Rosa exhibited six paintings. Her long-distance love affair with America probably began when she first encountered Catlin's work. She bought a book of his engravings and avidly copied them.

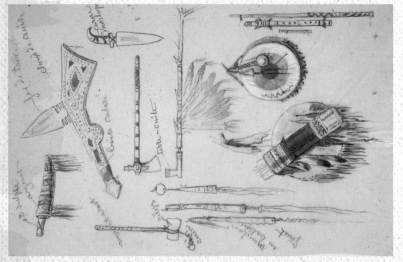

*Indian Artifacts, Weapons and Pipes*, after 1841. Rosa's drawing of tools and weapons copied from those of George Catlin.

*Stu-mick-o-súcks* (Buffalo Bull's Back Fat), 1832, by George Catlin. This portrait of a Blackfoot chief of the northern plains was shown at the 1846 Paris Salon.

*The Duel*, 1895. Critics claimed Rosa painted like a scientist when they saw this remarkably realistic image of fiery stallions fighting. Rosa's study of horses' anatomy had paid off.

# Bulls and Horses

In 1845, Rosa decided she wanted to understand how animals' bodies were made so that she could draw and paint them better. To study their anatomy, she went to a Parisian slaughterhouse! She watched and sketched as cows, pigs, goats, and horses were butchered, learning as much as she could about the animals' organs, bones, and muscles. This petite young woman intent on her drawing was a strange sight to the men who worked in the slaughterhouse. Some of them made fun of her, as the students at the Louvre had. "But when our aims are right, we always find help," Rosa wrote. "Providence sent me a protector in the good Monsieur Emile, a butcher of great physical strength." The muscular Monsieur Emile told the other men that if they bothered Rosa, they would have to answer to him. So Rosa was free to wander and sketch at the slaughterhouse undisturbed.

*Sketch of Five Bulls with Color Notes,* date unknown

The following year, Rosa went off on her first travel adventure: a three-hundred-mile trip through the rough countryside to the mountains of the Auvergne in central France. Farming was difficult in the hilly region, so men and animals had to work hard to cultivate the rocky soil. Rosa worked hard, too, to draw and paint what she saw there.

In 1848, Rosa was again invited to participate in the Paris Salon. There she exhibited *Cows and Bulls of the Cantal.* It was a triumph, winning her first gold medal at the Paris Salon. The well-known painters Eugène Delacroix and Jean-Baptiste-Camille Corot were among the judges who selected Rosa's painting for the award. *Cows and Bulls of the Cantal* brought widespread attention to Rosa's work, and she received a commission to create a painting about farming for the French government.

*Portrait of George Sand,* 1838, by Auguste Charpentier

*Plowing in the Nivernais,* 1849. This painting may have been inspired by the opening scene of the novel *The Devil's Pool* by George Sand. Rosa admired George Sand, a Frenchwoman who wrote under a man's name.

The resulting work, *Plowing in the Nivernais*, was a large painting, nearly four feet high and eight feet wide (260 cm x 133 cm). Rosa struggled to complete the commission the next year. Her final image of men and animals working together under a bright blue sky is an absolute sensation. Although two humans appear in the painting, the animals take center stage, their smooth coats contrasting with the rough texture of the rich, plowed earth. Rosa was proud of *Ploughing in the Nivernais* and painted several copies of it. It became one of her best-known paintings and was hung in the famous royal Palace of Fontainebleau. Finally, one critic paid the twenty-seven-year-old artist what he may have considered to be the ultimate compliment: "She paints like a man."

Rosa's studio, 1862. Illustrator unknown. It looked like, and probably smelled like, a barn!

In 1849, Rosa's father died. Rosa, who had been so close to him, was devastated. Raymond had been teaching at an art school that had been established for previously untutored female students. To honor her father's memory, Rosa promptly took over as director of the school. Her sister, Juliette, came to teach there, too. The students were a little bit afraid of Rosa, because she worked them hard and could be harsh in her criticism. "I have no patience with women who ask permission to think," Rosa once said. Although by now she had an ambitious painting schedule of her own and was successful enough not to need the income from running the school, Rosa continued to teach there for eleven years. She charitably longed to pass on to other women all that she had learned. "Ah, if only the world's nations could come together and use their resources for . . . educating their daughters, what happy changes would be, what an explosion of joy all over the earth! This is my dream, my obsession."

*Nathalie Micas,* 1850

R osa found it lonely at home after her father died, and she soon moved in with a childhood friend, Nathalie Micas, who also painted. Rosa had gotten to know Nathalie as a teenager, when Raymond had painted the girl's portrait. Nathalie's parents were fond of Rosa and treated her like a second daughter. Madame Micas even found a new art studio for the young women. This new studio included stable space for Rosa's four-footed models. She and Nathalie spent their days there, and Nathalie began assisting Rosa, painting in details and backgrounds, as Juliette and Auguste had also begun to do. Isidore and Rosa worked together to create sculptures, too. In 1850, Rosa and Nathalie decided to take a trip to the Pyrenees mountain range near Spain. There they rode wild donkeys, hunted vultures, had a grand adventure, and became friends for life.

*Spanish Muleteers Crossing the Pyrenees,* 1857

When she returned to Paris, Rosa bought a mare she named Margot. Most people thought women shouldn't ride horses, but, once again, Rosa simply didn't care what most people thought. She rode Margot in Paris every day and kept her at the studio's stable. Now Rosa began to plan a new painting, a HUGE one. She would paint horses—big, stamping, rearing, prancing horses!

To learn still more about the bodies and movements of the big animals, Rosa needed to go to the Paris horse fair, where men bought and sold horses, the main form of transportation in those days. The problem was, women were not welcome at the horse fair. So, beginning in 1851, Rosa began disguising herself as a boy. She put on pants and tucked her hair into a cap. It was against the law in France to dress in public as a member of the opposite sex. Rosa had to get a special permit from the police showing that she had a good reason to dress as a male. Permits like this were rarely issued, they had to be signed by a doctor, and they were good for only six months.

"This costume was a real protection to me," said Rosa. It meant she could stay at the horse fair all day long without being bothered. Rosa sketched the horses' oval eyes, their silky forelocks, their muscled haunches. "It's my dream to show the horses snorting fire and dust swelling up around their hooves," she wrote later. "I want this wild tornado to make people's heads spin!"

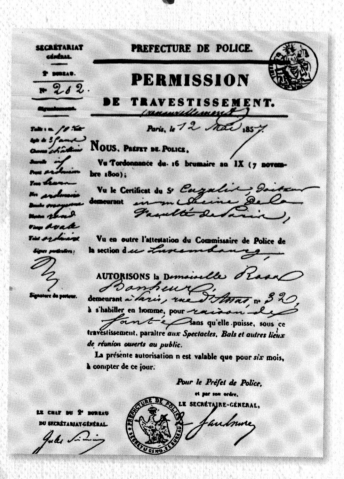

A document from the Paris police giving Rosa permission to dress as a man

*Studies for* The Horse Fair, *1852–1855*

*The Horse Fair*, 1852–1855. Rosa, who was not quite five feet tall, had to stand on a ladder day after day to paint this enormous work of art. It measures 8 feet tall by 16½ feet wide (244.5 x 506.7 cm)! Despite the painting's size, no details were left out. The dust around the horses' hooves, for example, is clearly visible. Many who see the painting at the Metropolitan Museum of Art in New York City today claim that it seems so real that you can almost hear hooves pounding.

Rosa Bonheur doll. This china doll was manufactured in Germany. It is part of a collection of nineteenth-century portrait dolls, representing popular characters from history.

For a year and a half, Rosa studied and sketched horses and their handlers. When her huge painting, *The Horse Fair*, was finished, it took up almost an entire wall at the 1853 Salon! People were amazed by it. Rosa had painted an image that represented three or four miles of space. Men and animals spun by in a whirlwind. Rosa dazzled everyone by revealing not only all she knew about anatomy and painting light and dark and movement and perspective, but also all she knew about every style of painting: Neo-Classicism, Romanticism, and Realism. *The Horse Fair* showed its subjects in many different positions, expressing many different attitudes, and passing through many different kinds of light. The painting was so sensational, some doubted that a woman could possibly have created it; they thought that only a man could paint something so powerful.

Ernest Gambart, a Belgian agent with a London office, purchased *The Horse Fair* and set about promoting the painting in Great Britain. Rosa made a smaller copy of the painting, and Gambart had prints made of it. Dubbed "The World's Greatest Animal Picture," its prints were sold all over Britain, Europe, and America. Copies were hung in many public places, including schoolrooms, and Rosa became a celebrity. A Rosa Bonheur doll began to be manufactured in Germany and became a popular toy. Everyone was fascinated by this spunky little woman with short hair who painted wearing pants. Even Queen Victoria wanted to meet her. At the queen's request, Gambart arranged for *The Horse Fair* to be brought to her at Windsor Castle for a private viewing.

*Bull with Raised Head,* date unknown

*A Sheep at Rest*, date unknown

# Sheep, Oxen, and Deer

Rosa's skyrocketing success enabled her to acquire an even bigger art studio. This one had a huge window looking out on a courtyard, its own garden, and fenced stables for her heifer, goats, sheep, and Margot, the mare. Rosa was creating her own small farm in the middle of Paris!

In 1856, Ernest Gambart decided that the time was right for Rosa herself to take a triumphal tour of Britain. Rosa was eager to see firsthand British animal paintings, which were popular at the time, but was worried because she could not speak a word of English. When the agent offered to act as her translator and escort, she and Nathalie packed their bags. Gambart convinced Sir Charles Eastlake, the president of Britain's Royal Academy of Arts at the time and a famous architect and furniture designer, to give a grand dinner in Rosa's honor. Because the Royal Academy was founded to promote the arts, many distinguished guests were invited to the banquet, including the well-known British animal painter Edwin Landseer and John Ruskin, the leading art critic of the time. Landseer was one of Rosa's heroes. She was so overcome when he presented her with two engravings that she burst into tears.

ambart also took Rosa and Nathalie to see the herds of deer at Windsor Park outside London, and to the city of Birmingham, where *The Horse Fair* was on display. Everywhere they went, the group met enthusiastic art lovers who wanted to buy Rosa's work. However, the highlight of the trip for Rosa was when they visited the Highlands of Scotland. "I love the Scotch mists, the cloud-swept mountains, the dark heather . . . I love them with all my heart!" the artist wrote. But, of course, being Rosa, she loved the sheep and oxen she saw in Scotland even more.

*The Highland Shepherd, 1959*

*Highland Raid,* 1860. Rosa witnessed a wild stampede during her visit to Scotland. But instead of running away like most people would do, the artist climbed up on top of a wagon and sketched the rampaging animals. ("Raid" is Old Scottish for "road.")

She simply had to take some home, so she went to the Falkirk Fair and bought seven oxen. She had already bought five Scottish sheep. Nathalie returned a bit early to Paris to make room for the oxen at Rosa's studio, but the customs people refused to let the animals enter France. "I had to give up and resell in England the beautiful beasts I was so proud of," Rosa wrote with regret. Nevertheless, Rosa never forgot Scotland. "My sketches were useful for years to come. They helped me out with *Stampede of Scottish Oxen, Oxen in the Highlands, Crossing Loch Loden, The Boat, The Razzia,* and several other major paintings."

*Study of a Dog,* c. 1860s. Rosa liked to paint her many dogs.

Ernest Gambart eventually sold *The Horse Fair* to an American collector. Back home in Paris, more and more people were eager to buy Rosa Bonheur's paintings. Now that she was famous, other celebrities wanted to meet her. Rosa enjoyed the attention at first but soon decided she needed more time to paint. So in 1859 she bought a large, "fairy-tale" country house, or château, near what could almost be described as an enchanted forest outside Paris. Rosa went to live in the Château de By with Nathalie, Nathalie's mother, and her many pets. She also acquired an otter, a stag, a gazelle, wild boars, monkeys, an eagle, and three wild horses, along with sixty cages of birds and plenty of dogs . . . her own private menagerie!

The Château de By in Thoméry, Rosa's longtime home as it appears today

Rosa Bonheur could never get enough of nature. She called it her teacher. She loved spending days painting in the nearby Forest of Fontainebleau. It was where she felt most at home. Rosa sometimes invited other artists to paint with her there; she generously wanted to share her bliss with them. "Be kind enough to think of me as an old friend or a sister," she wrote to painter and illustrator Paul Chardin, who became a lifelong friend. "Please come as often as you like to show me your studies, and don't ever worry about disturbing me." Sometimes Rosa even camped out in the forest for several nights at a time, watching the changing light and the habits of the animals that lived there. "Fontainebleau Forest in winter is beauty in perfection, with its long avenues of pure untrodden snow, save for the small hoofprints of the deer."

*Deer in the Forest of Fontainebleau, 1862*

Rosa Bonheur could never get enough of nature.
She called it her teacher.

One day in 1864 when she was in her studio working on a painting set in the forest, a maid came rushing in to tell Rosa that the Empress Eugénie had arrived to pay her a visit. The empress, wife of French Emperor Louis-Napoléon Bonaparte, was very impressed with Rosa's work. When she returned on a second visit to the studio a year later, she gave Rosa France's highest award, the *Légion d'Honneur*. It was the first time this medal had ever been awarded to a woman. Rosa wore it proudly and often, pinned over her heart.

During these happy, productive years, Rosa never forgot her family or what it had been like to live in poverty. She wrote to her brothers and sister constantly and helped educate her nieces and nephew. She was generous to outsiders, too. Once she was invited to a dinner where she met a young bride who mentioned that she and her husband could not entertain because they had no money to buy furniture. After dinner, Rosa asked for a piece of drawing paper. On it she sketched a hunting scene. She then handed the drawing to the young woman. "Give this to Tedesco [a Parisian art dealer] on your return to Paris, and he will give you at least fifteen hundred francs for it. Then you will be able to furnish your drawing room."

Louis-Napoléon and Empress Eugénie, c. 1865, by André-Adolphe-Eugène Disdéri. The empress encouraged her husband to bestow on Rosa the first *Légion d'Honneur* medal ever awarded to a woman.

Rosa's studio at the Château de By today

*Impression, Sunrise*, 1872, by Claude Monet. This is the painting that gave its name to Impressionism. The hazy, unfinished appearance and vivid color set Monet's painting of the port of Le Havre apart from more traditional, realistic paintings.

# Lions, Tigers, and Wild Horses

In spite of her popularity and success, not everyone liked Rosa's style of painting. A new movement called Impressionism was developing among some artists in France. Its goal was to show an artist's feeling or personal impression of a subject, not to create an accurate image.

The artist Paul Cézanne, who was closely linked with Impressionism, was asked his opinion of *Plowing in the Nivernais*. "It is horribly like the real thing," he said. But Rosa believed in honesty in art. For her, that meant keeping close to nature and faithfully representing it. She was happy with what she did and seemed neither to envy other artists nor feel the need to copy them. "Every kind of painting has its [own] masterpiece," she said.

In 1870, the French Emperor Louis-Napoléon Bonaparte declared war on Prussia, even though he had a smaller army and fewer weapons. Napoléon's soldiers, one of whom was Rosa's brother Auguste, lost battle after battle. Soon the Prussians had invaded France and were heading for Paris. Rosa was worried about her brother and wanted to be in the fight. She joined the home guard in the village of By and learned to shoot a musket. When the Prussians reached the countryside around Fontainebleau, Rosa tried to lead the villagers in an attack on the invaders. But no one thought it was a good idea; they did not want the Prussians to burn their village. The mayor told Rosa to go home, that she could not be "a new Joan of Arc." Disappointed, Rosa followed orders. When Paris fell, Louis-Napoléon was captured, and the war ended. Auguste survived, and Rosa went back to painting.

After the war, Rosa was invited to the home of a man who owned a circus. He had a lioness he wanted her to see. The lioness was Pierrette, who offered a paw to Rosa in greeting. It was love at first sight! Pierrette came to live with the artist at her château. Rosa's painting of her was the first of her many paintings of exotic animals. She soon began visiting circuses and zoos to study tigers, leopards, and monkeys. Before long she had acquired two more lions, Nero and Fathma, who played with her like giant house cats.

*Two Tigers, 1887*

*Lion Head,* 1879

In 1889, Nathalie, whose health had always been fragile, fell gravely ill. Rosa took tender care of her until she died later that year. Rosa buried her in the elegant Père Lachaise Cemetery in Paris. "Her loss broke my heart," the artist wrote. Nathalie's mother, Madame Micas, had passed away in 1875, so now Rosa was alone in her château except for her servants. For an entire summer the artist was so grief-stricken that she was unable to paint. But in September, Rosa was lured back into life by a visit to an exhibition that was the talk of Paris: Buffalo Bill's Wild West.

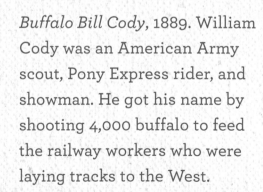

*Buffalo Bill Cody*, 1889. William Cody was an American Army scout, Pony Express rider, and showman. He got his name by shooting 4,000 buffalo to feed the railway workers who were laying tracks to the West.

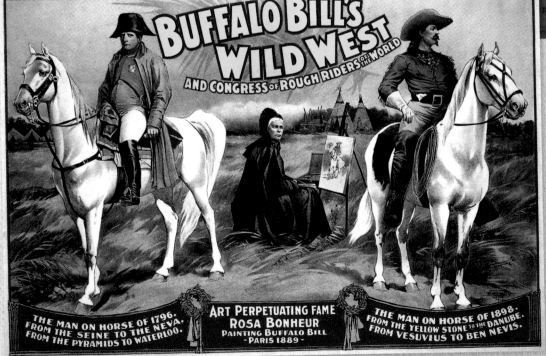

Poster for the Wild West show. Rosa is shown at her easel.

The famous American sharpshooter and cowboy William Frederick Cody had brought wild horses, buffalo, and a whole village of Native Americans to Paris . . . and Rosa lost herself in all these wonders! "Observing them [the performers] at close range really refreshed my sad old mind," she wrote. Rosa loved the Wild West show so much that she went nearly every day. She spent weeks sketching people and animals at the thirty-acre campground near a forest to the west of Paris, the Bois de Boulogne. She and Buffalo Bill became fast friends. He came to visit her at her château and gave her a pony and a beaded buckskin shirt. She painted a portrait of him on his horse, and it became one of his most prized possessions. He sent the portrait home to his wife in Nebraska for safekeeping. Later, when he learned that his house was on fire, he was said to have wired his wife: "Save the Rosa Bonheur, and let the flames take the rest." Although the fire would surely have died out long before Mrs. Cody received her husband's telegram, the message conveys just how much Buffalo Bill Cody loved Rosa's painting.

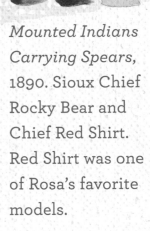

*Mounted Indians Carrying Spears,* 1890. Sioux Chief Rocky Bear and Chief Red Shirt. Red Shirt was one of Rosa's favorite models.

For the rest of her life, Rosa used the sketches she'd made of the people and animals at the Wild West show to create new paintings. Although she never visited the United States, she sold many of these Wild West–themed paintings to American clients. Two of the best known are *Buffalo Hunt* (1889) and *Mounted Indians Carrying Spears* (1890).

Buffalo Bill and Rosa with Chief Rocky Bear, Chief Red Shirt, Bronco Bill, and others at the 1899 Wild West show.

At about this time Rosa also made another important American friend through Wyoming horse dealer John Arbuckle. On a visit to Rosa in 1889, Arbuckle brought the young American artist Anna Klumpke to act as a translator. Anna was thrilled to meet Rosa—as a child she had treasured her Rosa Bonheur doll! Over time, the two artists became trusted friends. Rosa encouraged Anna in her career and graciously gave the younger woman permission to paint several portraits of her. She also asked her to write her "autobiography," which Anna did. The two women developed a deep affection for each other and began to share their lives. Together, they often took drives and painted in the Forest of Fontainebleau. Together, they also exhibited paintings and visited the Salon of 1899. Rosa died of a brief illness later that year, with Anna at her side.

*Rosa Bonheur*, 1898, by Anna Klumpke. In this portrait, Rosa's *Légion d'Honneur* medal can be seen on her jacket.

*Rosa Bonheur,* 1857, by Èdouard Louis Dubufe. As seen in this portrait, Rosa did not always wear pants. She often wore skirts and dresses when she was not working.

# Epilogue

Rosa Bonheur (1822–1899) was, in her day, the most famous female painter in the world. Another French painter, Édouard Louis Dubufe, created a portrait of her. In the original work, Rosa's arm rested on a table. She thought that was dull, so she asked Dubufe if she could paint a bull where the table was. When Dubufe sold the resulting painting to a collector, Rosa was paid a bonus, because the collector thought the bull was the best part of the artwork!

As we know from Rosa's story, it was difficult for a girl to become an artist in the 1800s. Two years before Rosa died in 1899, ten women were finally allowed into the best art school in Paris. But even then they were not permitted to paint or take life-drawing classes with men until the beginning of the twentieth century. Many women gave up on trying to become artists, but not Rosa. During her seventy-seven years, she created hundreds of wildlife paintings. Rosa's masterpiece, *The Horse Fair,* is hung at the Metropolitan Museum of Art in New York. The Met guidebook calls it "one of the museum's most popular and best-loved paintings."

Almost all the humans in *The Horse Fair* are concentrating on the galloping, stamping, and rearing horses. But one figure near the very center of the painting, wearing a blue jacket and a dark cap, holds a horse's reins in confident hands and, half smiling, looks calmly out at the viewer. Some say that this figure is Rosa herself, that she painted her own portrait (perhaps disguised as a male, as she was when she made her studies for the painting) into this lively scene. Another story is that the small brown riderless horse toward the left in the painting represents Rosa, a woman who did not allow others to manage or control her.

*Bonheur* means *happiness* in French.

Detail of *The Horse Fair* showing Rosa's purported self-portrait

# Author's Note

My home is three blocks away from the Metropolitan Museum of Art in New York City. Some days, I stroll through the museum until I discover one work of art I want to spend time studying. One day, while walking through the European paintings and sculptures, a huge painting caught my eye. The painting was a dramatic scene of powerful horses parading by. Despite the painting's monumental size, no detail was lacking. The horse's eyes glinted; the dust kicked up by their hooves was suspended in the air. I was captivated. I studied the painting for some time, then read the attribution. *The Horse Fair* was created in the nineteenth century by a woman, Rosa Bonheur. Because a single female would attract negative attention at a place like the horse fair in Paris, the artist had dressed like a man to be able to make preparatory sketches for her painting. Here was a story!

I began reading about Rosa in the museum's library. The more I read, the more excited I became about writing her biography for children. I learned that Rosa came from a poor family, and that because of her gender she was denied a formal art education. Despite this, she became the most famous female artist of her day. She never allowed her inability to study human anatomy in art school to hold her back. Instead, she sketched and painted what she loved best: animals of all kinds. Rosa lived life her own way, refusing to follow the trends of the day in art or in fashion. She made use of her skills and fortune to help others, too. Rosa was someone I wanted to get to know.

I planned a journey to France, to follow as best I could in Rosa's footsteps. I visited the street in the Marais in Paris where Rosa lived as a child and spent time admiring one of her masterpieces,

Rosa's palette, decorated with a stag

*Plowing in the Nivernais*, at the Musée d'Orsay. I visited the neighborhood where she studied anatomy in a slaughterhouse. But despite my best efforts, I was unable to arrange a visit to Rosa's château in Thoméry, near Fontainebleau. The château, which had become a museum, was temporarily closed. I was disappointed, but decided to return when and if the museum reopened.

Back in New York, I read everything I could find about Rosa and her talented family. She created hundreds of animal paintings and sculptures in her lifetime. I collected some of my favorite images and wrote a picture book text to go with them. My agent, Steven Chudney, introduced me to Abrams editor Howard Reeves, who encouraged me to expand my book for older readers.

I did more research, discovering the many twists and turns in Rosa's life and art and meeting more enthusiastic and helpful people along the way. Through a librarian at the Watson Library at the Metropolitan Museum of Art, I learned that an art historian had created a catalog, or *catalogue raisonné* (a comprehensive listing) of Rosa's work. That art historian's name was Annie-Paule Quinsac. After some searching, I found her telephone number. I took a deep breath and dialed it before I lost my nerve. Ms. Quinsac answered and generously invited me to her home in the Bronx, not far from mine in Manhattan, for tea. In her quiet apartment filled with nineteenth-century paintings, she showed me her own two Rosa Bonheurs, discussed the artist and her place in history, and shared news about Rosa's château. A sale was underway, she told me, but it was unlikely to be concluded for some months. In the meantime, there was no access to the château, Rosa's studio, or any of the treasures within.

Although it was impossible to visit the château, the tourist bureau in Thoméry sent me some wonderful photos of it. Another art historian, Alessandra Comini in Texas, provided a digital image of her own painting by Rosa, *Ewe at Rest*, for use in the book. Some of the artworks were easy to locate; others took some detective work. I very much wanted to find an image of a Rosa Bonheur doll. I contacted doll and toy museums across the country with no success. Finally, the curator at the Doll Museum at the Old Rectory in Worthington, Ohio, came to the rescue, sending a snapshot of the Rosa Bonheur doll in its collection.

Despite her fame, Rosa's popularity dimmed after her life ended. The influence of the Impressionists surpassed that of the Realists who had preceded them, and Rosa was largely dismissed and forgotten. But popular or not, I doubt this artist would ever have regretted the path she took. She found all the beauty and truth she sought by staying close to nature in her art and her life.

# Notes

Page 5 "Fathma . . . followed me around like a poodle": Klumpke, *Rosa Bonheur*, 184.

Page 5 "To be loved by wild animals": Stanton, *Reminiscences of Rosa Bonheur*, 338.

Page 7 "You just cannot imagine": Klumpke, *Rosa Bonheur*, 87.

Page 7 "Rosa is a dear little thing": Stanton, *Reminiscences of Rosa Bonheur*, 13.

Page 7 "I don't know what Rosa will be": Ibid.

Page 8 "Rosalie asks every day": Ibid.

Page 8 "Rosalie is sending you": Ibid.

Page 8 "I thought he was alive": Ibid., 89.

Page 11 "This was, I believe": Ibid., 7.

Page 12 "My mother, the most noble": Klumpke, *Rosa Bonheur*, 102–103.

Page 12 "I was a real devil there": Ibid., 106.

Page 12 "At long last I was going to be able": Ibid., 110 (similar).

Page 16 "I have never seen . . . such ardor for work": Ellet, *Women Artists*, 82.

Page 16 "What a joy": Klumpke, *Rosa Bonheur*, 113.

Page 20 "I really got into studying their ways": Ibid., 122.

Page 20 "Always begin with a vision": Klumpke, *Rosa Bonheur*, 219.

Page 27 "But when our aims are right": Ibid., tk.

Page 29 "She paints like a man": Ashton, *Rosa Bonheur: A Life and a Legend*, 51.

Page 30 "I have no patience": Stanton, *Reminiscences of Rosa Bonheur*, 63.

Page 30 "Ah, if only all the world's nations": Klumpke, *Rosa Bonheur*, 197.

Page 32 "This costume was a real protection": Stanton, *Reminiscences of Rosa Bonheur*, 85.

Page 32 "It's my dream": Klumpke, *Rosa Bonheur*, 217

Page 40 "I love the Scotch mists": Stanton, *Reminiscences of Rosa Bonheur*, 136.

Page 41 "I had to give up and resell": Klumpke, *Rosa Bonheur*, 159.

Page 41 "My sketches were useful": Ibid., 152.

Page 44 "Be kind enough to think of me": Urbanek, *Rosa Bonheur: Selected Works from American Collections* (unpaged).

Page 44 "Fontainebleau Forest in winter": Ashton, *Rosa Bonheur: A Life and a Legend*, 119.

Page 46 "Give this to Tedesco": Stanton, *Reminiscences of Rosa Bonheur*, 396.

Page 49 "It is horribly like the real thing": Ashton, *Rosa Bonheur: A Life and a Legend*, 70.

Page 49 "Every kind of painting has its masterpiece": Stanton, *Reminiscences of Rosa Bonheur*, 376.

Page 50 "I couldn't be a new Joan of Arc": Klumpke, *Rosa Bonheur*, xxxiv.

Page 52 "Her loss broke my heart": Stanton, Reminiscences of *Rosa Bonheur*, 121.

Page 53 "Observing them at close range": Klumpke, *Rosa Bonheur*, 293.

Page 53 "Save the Rosa Bonheur": Ashton, *Rosa Bonheur: A Life and a Legend*, 155.

# Bibliography

Ashton, Dore, and Denise Browne Hare. *Rosa Bonheur: A Life and a Legend*. New York: Viking Press, 1981.

Ellet, Elizabeth Fries. *Women Artists in All Ages and Countries*. New York: Harper and Bros., 1859.

Klumpke, Anna. *Rosa Bonheur*. Ann Arbor: The University of Michigan Press, 2001.

Metropolitan Museum of Art Guide. New York: Metropolitan Museum of Art (distributed by Yale University Press). Undated.

Reese, Jennifer Tesoro. *Six Women, Six Stories*. New York: Metropolitan Museum of Art (Family Guide), 2011.

*Rosa Bonheur: All Nature's Children*. New York: Dahesh Museum (exhibition catalog), 1998.

*Rosa Bonheur: Selected Works from American Collections*. Dallas: Meadows Museum, Southern Methodist University (exhibition catalog), 1989.

Stanton, Theodore. *Reminiscences of Rosa Bonheur*. London: Andrew Melrose, 1910.

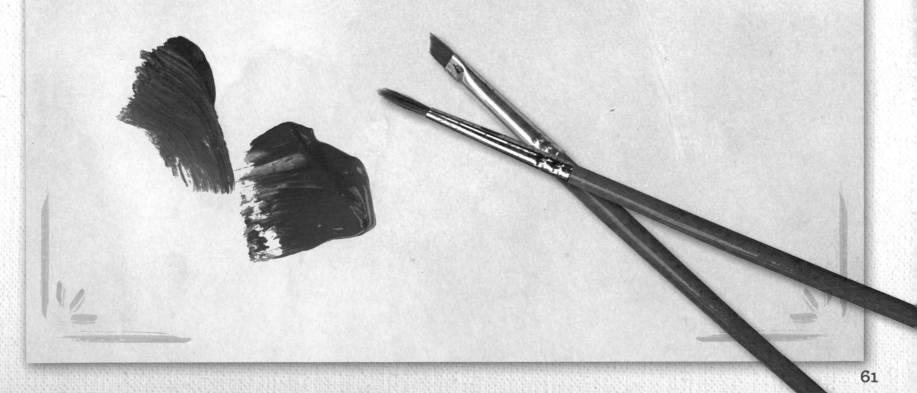

# Where to See Rosa Bonheur's Work

**UNITED STATES**

Art Institute of Chicago, Illinois
Bowdoin College Museum of Art, Maine
Brooklyn Museum, New York
Buffalo Bill Museum, Wyoming
Cleveland Museum of Art, Ohio
Dahesh Museum of Art, New York
Detroit Institute of Arts, Michigan
Fine Arts Museums of San Francisco,
        California
Haggin Museum, California
Indianapolis Museum of Art, Indiana
John and Mable Ringling Museum of Art,
        Florida
Metropolitan Museum of Art, New York
Minneapolis Institute of Art, Minnesota
National Museum of Wildlife Art,
        Wyoming
National Museum of Women in the Arts,
        Washington, D.C.
Philadelphia Museum of Art, Pennsylvania
Princeton University Art Museum,
        New Jersey
Walters Art Museum, Maryland

**OTHER COUNTRIES**

Art Gallery of Ontario, Toronto, Ontario,
        Canada
Bilbao Fine Arts Museum, Bilbao, Spain
Ferens Art Gallery, Hull, England
Kunsthalle Hamburg, Hamburg, Germany
Louvre Museum, Paris, France
Musée des Beaux Arts, Bordeaux, France
Musée d'Orsay, Paris, France
Musée Nationale du Chateau de
        Fontainebleau, Fontainebleau, France
National Gallery, London, England
Prado Museum, Madrid, Spain
Walker Art Gallery, Liverpool, England
Wallace Collection, Marylebone, England

# Acknowledgments

I am grateful to Steven Chudney, my agent, whose good judgment led me to Howard Reeves, an editor of intelligence and restraint. Howard's vision helped give shape to this book. I am also grateful to Christel Leboeuf at the Mairie de Thoméry and to retired professors Alessandra Comini and Annie-Paule Quinsac for their patient assistance in my search for illustrations. Thanks goes, too, to my husband, George, whose enthusiasm always helps carry me along, and to my daughter, Alison, for her patient technical support.

# Image Credits

*All artwork by Rosa Bonheur unless otherwise credited.*

Page 4: *The Lion at Home*, 1881. Ferens Art Gallery, Hull Museums, UK. Page 6: *Rosa at Four*, 1826, by Raymond Bonheur. Château de By. Page 8: *A horse-drawn bus in Paris*, 1828. Illustrator unknown. State Library of Victoria. Page 9: *Boulevard du Temple*, 1838–1889, by Louis Dauguerre. Page 10: *The Saint-Simonians Get Dressed.* Illustrator and date unknown. Bibliotéque nationale de Paris. Page 12: *Drawing of a horse*, 1835. Princeton University Library. Page 13: *Self-portrait,* 1823, by Raymond Bonheur. Musée des Beaux-Arts, Bordeaux. Page 14: *Rabbits Nibbling Carrots*, detail, 1840. Page 16: Louvre Museum, c. 1865, by Auguste-Rosalie Bisson. Museum of Photographic Arts, San Diego. Page 16: Cartoon of a copyist, 1836. Page 17: (*left*) *Joan of Arc at the Coronation of Charles VII*, 1854, by Jean-Auguste-Dominique Ingres. Louvre Museum; (*right*) *Confrontation of Knights in the Countryside*, 1834–1842, by Eugene Delacroix. Louvre Museum. Page 18: *A Ewe and Two Lambs*, date unknown, Juliette Bonheur. Page 19: (*left*) The Bonheur family, c. 1860s, by André-Alphonse-Eugene Disideri. National Portrait Gallery, London; (*right*) *Goat*, date unknown, Isidore Bonheur. Page 21: *Head of a Calf*, 1878. Bonham's. Musée des Beaux-Arts, Bordeaux. Page 22: *Rabbits Nibbling Carrots*, 1840. Musée des Beaux-Arts, Bordeaux. Page 23: Salon de Paris, 1857. Musée Carnavalet. Page 24: (*top*) *George Catlin*, 1849, William Fisk; (*bottom*) *Indian Artifacts, Weapons and Pipes*, after 1841. Whitney Gallery of Western Art. Page 25: *Stu-Mick-o-súcks (Buffalo Bull's Back Fat)*, 1832, by George Catlin. Smithsonian American Art Museum. Page 26: *The Duel*, Rosa Bonheur, 1895. Page 28: (*top*) *Sketch of Five Bulls with Color Notes*, date unknown. Walters Art Museum; (*bottom*) *Portrait of George Sand,* 1938. Musée de la Vie Romantique. Page 29: *Plowing in the Nivernais*, 1849. Musée d'Orsay. Page 30: Rosa Bonheur's Studio, 1862. Page 31: (*top*) *Natalie Micas*, 1850. Château de By. New York Public Library; (*bottom*) *Spanish Muleteers Crossing the Pyrenees*, 1857. Sotheby's. Page 32: *Permission de Travestissement*, 1862. Préfecture de Police de Paris; *Studies for the Horse Fair,* 1852–1855. Pages 34–35: *The Horse Fair*, 1852–55. Metropolitan Museum of Art. Page 36: Rosa Bonheur doll. Doll Museum at the Old Rectory, Worthington, Ohio. Page 37: *Bull with Raised Head,* date unknown. University of Texas at Austin. Page 38: *A Sheep at Rest,* date unknown. Collection of Dr. Alessandra Comini. Page 40: *The Highland Shepherd*, 1859. Kunsthalle Hamburg. Page 41: Highland Raid, 1860. National Museum of Women in the Arts. Page 42: *Study of a Dog*, c. 1860s. Princeton University Art Museum. Page 44: Château de By today, date unknown. Maire de Thoméry. Page 45: *Deer in the Forest of Fontainebleau*, 1862. Page 46: Louis Napoleon and Empress Eugenie. Metropolitan Museum of Art. Page 47: Rosa's studio at the Château de By today, date unknown. Mairie de Thoméry. Page 48: *Impression, Sunrise*, 1872, by Claude Monet. Musée Marmottan. Page 50: *Two Tigers*, 1887, Rosa Bonheur. Keys Auctioneers. Page 51: *Lion Head*, 1879, Rosa Bonheur. Prado Museum. Page 52: (*top right*) *Buffalo Bill Cody*, 1889. Whitney Gallery of Western Art; (*bottom left*) *Buffalo Bill's Wild West and Congress of Rough Riders of the World*, c. 1896. Illustrator unknown. Courier Litho. Co., Buffalo, NY. Library of Congress. Page 53: *Mounted Indians Carrying Spears*, 1890. Whitney Gallery of Western Art. Page 54: Buffalo Bill and Rosa with Rocky Bear, Red Shirt, Bronco Bill, and others at 1899 Wild West show. Buffalo Bill Center of the West. Page 55: *Rosa Bonheur*, 1898, by Anna Klumke. Metropolitan Museum of Art. Page 56: *Rosa Bonheur*, 1857, by Louis Dubufe. Chateau de Versailles. Page 57: Detail of Horse Fair. Metropolitan Museum of Art. Page 58: Rosa Bonheur's palette. Minneapolis Museum of Art.

# Index

Note: Page numbers in *italics* designate reproduction of artworks.

Antin, Father, 11
Arbuckle, John, 54

*The Boat*, 41
Bonaparte, Louis-Napoléon, 46, *46*, 50
Bonheur, Auguste (brother), 8, 11, 18, 19, *19*, 31, 50
Bonheur, Isidore (brother), 8, 11, 18, 19, *19*, 31
Bonheur, Juliette (sister), 11, 18, *18*, 19, *19*, 30, 31
Bonheur, Raymond (father), 7, 8, 15, 18, 30
  Saint-Simonians and, 10, *10*, 11, 12
  works by, 6, *6*, 12, *13*
Bonheur, Rosalie "Rosa," 6, *6*, 19, *19*, 36, *36*, 52, *52*,
    54, *54*, 55, *55*, 56, *56*, 57, *57*. See also specific
    topics
Bonheur, Sophie (mother), 7, 8, 11, 12
*Boulevard du Temple*, 9, *9*
Bronco Bill, 54, *54*
Buffalo Bill, 52, *52*, 53, 54, *54*
*Buffalo Bull's Back Fat (Stu-mick-o-súcks)*, 25, *25*
*Buffalo Hunt*, 54
*Bull with Raised Head*, 37, *37*
By, 43, 44, *44*, 47, *47*, 59

Catlin, George, 24, *24*, 25, *25*
Cézanne, Paul, 49
Chardin, Paul, 44
Charpentier, Auguste, 28, *28*
Château de By, 43, 44, *44*, 47, *47*, 59
childhood, *6*, 7, 8, 11–12
Cody, William Frederick "Buffalo Bill," 52, *52*, 53, 54,
    *54*
*Confrontation of Knights in the Countryside*, 17, *17*
Corot, Jean-Baptiste-Camille, 28
*Cows and Bulls of the Cantal*, 28
cross-dressing, 32, *32*, 58
*Crossing Loch Loden*, 41

Daguerre, Louis, 9, *9*
*Deer in the Forest of Fontainebleau*, 45, *45*
Delacroix, Eugène, 17, *17*, 28
dolls, 7, *7*, 36, *36*, 59
Dubufe, Édouard Louis, 56, *56*, 57
*The Duel*, 26

Eastlake, Charles, 39
education, 11, 12, 15, 16, 18, *27*, 30
Emile, Monsieur, 27
Eugénie (Empress), 46, *46*
*A Ewe and Two Lambs*, 18, *18*

family, 7, 8, 11, 12, 18, 19, *19*, 30, 31, 50. See also
    Bonheur, Raymond
Fisk, William, 24, *24*
Fontainebleau, 29, 44, 45, *45*, 50, 54

Gambart, Ernest, 37, 39, 43
*George Catlin*, 24, *24*
*Goat*, 19, *19*

*Head of a Calf*, 21, *21*
*Highland Raid*, 41, *41*
*The Highland Shepherd*, 40, *40*
*The Horse Fair*, 33, *33*, 34, 35, *35*, 37, 40, 43, 57, *57*, 58

*Impression, Sunrise*, 48, *48*
Impressionists, 48, *48*, 49, 59
*Indian Artifacts, Weapons and Pipes*, 24, *24*
Ingres, Jean Auguste Dominique, 17, *17*

*Joan of Arc at the Coronation of Charles VII*, 17, *17*

Klumpke, Anna, 54, 55, *55*

Landseer, Edwin, 39
*Légion d'Honneur*, 46, 55, *55*
*The Lion at Home*, 4, *4*
*Lion Head*, 50, 51, *51*
Louvre Museum, 16, *16*, 23, *23*, 24, 25, *25*, 28, 37, 54

Metropolitan Museum of Art, 35, 57, 58, 59
Micas, Nathalie, 31, *31*, 39, 40, 43, 52
Monet, Claude, 48, *48*
*Mounted Indians Carrying Spears*, 53, *53*, 54

Native Americans, 24, *24*, 25, *25*, 53, *53*, 54, *54*
Neo-Classicism, 15, 17, *17*

*Oxen in the Highlands*, 41

Paris, 8, *8*, 9, *9*, 32, 52, 53, 58–59
  Louvre Museum in, 16, *16*, 23, *23*, 24, 25, *25*, 28,
    37, 54
*Plowing in the Nivernais*, 29, *29*, 49, 59
*Portrait of George Sand*, 28, *28*

*Rabbits Nibbling Carrots*, 14, *14*, 22, 23
*The Razzia*, 41
Realism, 15, 20, 59
Red Shirt (Chief), 53, *53*, 54, 54
Rocky Bear, 53, *53*
*Rosa at Four*, 6, *6*
*Rosa Bonheur* (1857), 56, *56*, 57
*Rosa Bonheur* (1898), 55, *55*
Royal Academy of Arts, 39
Ruskin, John, 39

Saint-Simonians, 10, *10*, 11, 12
Salon de Paris, 23, *23*, 24, 25, *25*, 28, 37, 54
Sand, George, 28, 29
Scotland, 40, *40*, 41, *41*
*Self-portrait* (Raymond), 12, *13*
*A Sheep at Rest*, 38, *38*
*Sketch of Five Bulls with Color Notes*, 28, *28*
*Spanish Muleteers Crossing the Pyrenees*, 31, *31*
*Stampede of Scottish Oxen*, 41
*Studies for The Horse Fair*, 33, *33*
*Study of a Dog*, 42, *42*
*Stu-mick-o-súcks (Buffalo Bull's Back Fat)*, 25, *25*

Tedesco (art dealer), 46
Thomery, 43, 44, *44*, 47, *47*, 59
*Two Tigers*, 50, *50*

United Kingdom, 37, 39, 40, 41

Victoria (Queen), 37

War of 1870, 50